Maya Angelou was born in 1928 in St Louis, Missouri. After the break-up of her parents' marriage she and her beloved brother Bailey went to live with their grandmother, whose general store was the centre of life for the Black communtiy in Stamps, Arkansas. At eight Maya was raped by her mother's boyfriend and for the next five years she became mute. In her teens she and Bailey moved to California to live with their mother in a world that offered sharp and memorable contrasts to that of Stamps. At sixteen, having just graduated from school, Maya gave birth to her son, Guy.

In the years that followed she has been waitress, singer, actress, dancer, Black activist, editor, as well as mother. She has had, as she describes it, "a roller coaster life . . . there has been this disappointment and that satisfaction, and then it begins all over again". In her twenties she toured Europe and Africa in *Porgy and Bess*. Moving to New York, she joined the Harlem Writers Guild and continued to earn her living as a night-club singer and performer in Genet's *The Blacks*. She became involved in Black struggles in the 1960s and then spent several years in Ghana as editor of *African Review*.

Maya Angelou has produced several collections of poetry of which *And Still I Rise* and *Just Give Me a Cool Drink of Water 'Fore I Diiie* have been published by Virago. With verse by Maya Angelou and illustrations by Tom Feelings, the two have collaborated in *Now Sheba Sings the Song* (Virago). The five volumes of her highly acclaimed autobiography, *I Know Why the Caged Bird Sings, Gather Together in My Name, Singin' and Swingin' and Gettin' Merry Like Christmas, The Heart of a Woman* and *All God's Children Need Travelling Shoes* are also published by Virago. Maya Angelou now has a life-time appointment as Reynolds Professor of American Studies at Wake Forest University in North Carolina.

ALSO BY MAYA ANGELOU

I Know Why the Caged Bird Sings
Gather Together In My Name
Singin' and Swingin' and Gettin' Merry Like Christmas
The Heart of a Woman
All God's Children Need Travelling Shoes
And Still I Rise
Just Give Me a Cool Drink of Water 'Fore I Diie
Now Sheba Sings the Song

MAYA ANGELOU

I SHALL

NOT BE

MOVED

VIRAGO

Published by VIRAGO PRESS Limited 1990
20–23 Mandela Street, Camden Town, London NW1 0HQ

First published in the USA by Random House, New York
and simultaneously in Canada by Random House of Canada
Limited, Toronto, 1990.

*A CIP catalogue record for this title
is available from the British Library*

Printed in Great Britain
by Cox and Wyman Ltd
Reading, Berkshire

VIVIAN BAXTER
MILDRED GARRIS TUTTLE

CONTENTS

I SHALL

NOT BE

MOVED

WORKER'S SONG

Big ships shudder
down to the sea
    because of me
Railroads run
on a twinness track
    'cause of my back
    Whoppa, Whoppa
    Whoppa, Whoppa

Cars stretch to a
super length
    'cause of my strength
Planes fly high
over seas and lands
    'cause of my hands
    Whoppa, Whoppa
    Whoppa, Whoppa

I wake
start the factory humming
I work late
keep the whole world running
and I got something . . . something
coming . . . coming. . . .
    Whoppa
    Whoppa
    Whoppa

HUMAN FAMILY

I note the obvious differences
in the human family.
Some of us are serious,
some thrive on comedy.

Some declare their lives are lived
as true profundity,
and others claim they really live
the real reality.

The variety of our skin tones
can confuse, bemuse, delight,
brown and pink and beige and purple,
tan and blue and white.

I've sailed upon the seven seas
and stopped in every land,
I've seen the wonders of the world,
not yet one common man.

I know ten thousand women
called Jane and Mary Jane,
but I've not seen any two
who really were the same.

Mirror twins are different
although their features jibe,
and lovers think quite different thoughts
while lying side by side.

We love and lose in China,
we weep on England's moors,
and laugh and moan in Guinea,
and thrive on Spanish shores.

We seek success in Finland,
are born and die in Maine.
In minor ways we differ,
in major we're the same.

I note the obvious differences
between each sort and type,
but we are more alike, my friends,
than we are unalike.

We are more alike, my friends,
than we are unalike.

We are more alike, my friends,
than we are unalike.

MAN BIGOT

The man who is a bigot
is the worst thing God has got,
except his match, his woman,
who really is Ms. Begot.

OLD FOLKS LAUGH

They have spent their
content of simpering,
holding their lips this
and that way, winding
the lines between
their brows. Old folks
allow their bellies to jiggle like slow
tamborines.
The hollers
rise up and spill
over any way they want.
When old folks laugh, they free the world.
They turn slowly, slyly knowing
the best and worst
of remembering.
Saliva glistens in
the corners of their mouths,
their heads wobble
on brittle necks, but
their laps
are filled with memories.
When old folks laugh, they consider the promise
of dear painless death, and generously
forgive life for happening
to them.

IS LOVE

Midwives and winding sheets
know birthing is hard
and dying is mean
and living's a trial in between.

Why do we journey, muttering
like rumors among the stars?
Is a dimension lost?
Is it love?

FORGIVE

Take me, Virginia,
bind me close
with Jamestown memories
of camptown races and
ships pregnant
with certain cargo
and Richmond riding high on greed
and low on tedious tides
of guilt.

But take me on, Virginia,
loose your turban of flowers
that peach petals and
dogwood bloom may
form epaulettes of white
tenderness on my shoulders
and round my
head ringlets
of forgiveness, poignant
as rolled eyes, sad as summer
parasols in a hurricane.

INSIGNIFICANT

A series of small, on
their own insignificant,
occurrences. Salt lost half
its savor. Two yellow-
striped bumblebees got
lost in my hair.
When I freed them they droned
away into the afternoon.

At the clinic the nurse's
face was half pity and part pride.
I was not glad for the news.
Then I thought I heard you
call, and I, running
like water, headed for
the railroad track. It was only
the Baltimore and the Atchison,
Topeka, and the Santa Fe.
Small insignificancies.

LOVE LETTER

Listening winds
overhear my privacies
spoken aloud (in your
absence, but for your sake).

When you, mustachioed,
nutmeg-brown lotus,
sit beside the Oberlin shoji.

My thoughts are particular:
of your light lips and hungry
hands writing Tai Chi urgencies
into my body. I leap, float,
run

to spring cool springs into
your embrace. Then we match grace.
This girl, neither feather nor
fan, drifted and tossed.

Oh, but then I had power.
Power.

EQUALITY

You declare you see me dimly
through a glass which will not shine,
though I stand before you boldly,
trim in rank and marking time.

You do own to hear me faintly
as a whisper out of range,
while my drums beat out the message
and the rhythms never change.

Equality, and I will be free.
Equality, and I will be free.

You announce my ways are wanton,
that I fly from man to man,
but if I'm just a shadow to you,
could you ever understand?

We have lived a painful history,
we know the shameful past,
but I keep on marching forward,
and you keep on coming last.

Equality, and I will be free.
Equality, and I will be free.

Take the blinders from your vision,
take the padding from your ears,

and confess you've heard me crying,
and admit you've seen my tears.

Hear the tempo so compelling,
hear the blood throb in my veins.
Yes, my drums are beating nightly,
and the rhythms never change.

Equality, and I will be free.
Equality, and I will be free.

COLERIDGE JACKSON

Coleridge Jackson had nothing
to fear. He weighed sixty pounds
more than his sons and one
hundred pounds more than his wife.

His neighbors knew he wouldn't
take tea for the fever.
The gents at the poolroom
walked gently in his presence.

So everyone used
to wonder why,
when his puny boss, a little
white bag of bones and
squinty eyes, when he frowned
at Coleridge, sneered at
the way Coleridge shifted
a ton of canned goods from
the east wall of the warehouse
all the way to the west,
when that skimpy piece of
man-meat called Coleridge
a sorry nigger,
Coleridge kept his lips closed,
sealed, jammed tight.
Wouldn't raise his eyes,
held his head at a slant,

looking way off somewhere
else.

Everybody in the neighborhood wondered
why Coleridge would come home,
pull off his jacket, take off
his shoes, and beat the
water and the will out of his puny
little family.

Everybody, even Coleridge, wondered
(the next day, or even later that
same night).
Everybody. But the weasly little
sack-of-bones boss with his
envious little eyes,
he knew. He always
knew. And
when people told him about
Coleridge's family, about the
black eyes and the bruised
faces, the broken bones,
Lord, how that scrawny man
grinned.

And the next
day, for a few hours, he treated
Coleridge nice. Like Coleridge
had just done him the biggest
old favor. Then, right
after lunch, he'd start on
Coleridge again.

"Here, Sambo, come here.
Can't you move any faster
than that? Who on earth
needs a lazy nigger?"
And Coleridge would just
stand there. His eyes sliding
away, lurking at something else.

WHY ARE THEY HAPPY PEOPLE?

Skin back your teeth, damn you,
wiggle your ears,
laugh while the years
race
down your face.

Pull up your cheeks, black boy,
wrinkle your nose,
grin as your toes
spade
up your grave.

Roll those big eyes, black gal,
rubber your knees,
smile when the trees
bend
with your kin.

SON TO MOTHER

I start no
wars, raining poison
on cathedrals,
melting Stars of David
into golden faucets
to be lighted by lamps
shaded by human skin.

I set no
store on the strange lands,
send no
missionaries beyond my
borders,
to plunder secrets
and barter souls.

They
say you took my manhood,
Momma.
Come sit on my lap
and tell me,
what do you want me to say
to them, just
before I annihilate
their ignorance?

KNOWN TO EVE AND ME

His tan and golden self,
coiled in a threadbare carapace,
beckoned to my sympathy.
I hoisted him, shoulders above
the crowded plaza, lifting
his cool, slick body toward the altar of
sunlight. He was guileless, and slid into my embrace.
We shared seeded rolls and breakfast on the
   mountaintop.
Love's warmth and Aton's sun
disc caressed
his skin, and once-dulled scales
became sugared ginger, amber
drops of beryl on the tongue.

His lidless eye slid sideways,
and he rose into my deepest
yearning, bringing
gifts of ready rhythms, and
hourly wound around
my chest,
holding me fast in taut
security.
Then, glistening like
diamonds strewn
upon a black girl's belly,
he left me. And nothing
remains. Beneath my left
breast, two perfect identical punctures,

through which I claim
the air I breathe and
the slithering sound of my own skin
moving in the dark.

THESE YET TO BE UNITED STATES

Tremors of your network
cause kings to disappear.
Your open mouth in anger
makes nations bow in fear.
Your bombs can change the seasons,
obliterate the spring.
What more do you long for?
Why are you suffering?

You control the human lives
in Rome and Timbuktu.
Lonely nomads wandering
owe Telstar to you.
Seas shift at your bidding,
your mushrooms fill the sky.
Why are you unhappy?
Why do your children cry?

They kneel alone in terror
with dread in every glance.
Their nights are threatened daily
by a grim inheritance.
You dwell in whitened castles
with deep and poisoned moats
and cannot hear the curses
which fill your children's throats.

ME AND MY WORK

I got a piece of a job on the waterfront.
Three days ain't hardly a grind.
It buys some beans and collard greens
and pays the rent on time.
                Course the wife works, too.

Got three big children to keep in school,
need clothes and shoes on their feet,
give them enough of the things they want
and keep them out of the street.
                They've always been good.

My story ain't news and it ain't all sad.
There's plenty worse off than me.
Yet the only thing I really don't need
is strangers' sympathy.
That's someone else's word for
                caring.

CHANGING

It occurs to me now,
I never see you smiling
anymore. Friends
praise your
humor rich, your phrases
turning on a thin
dime. For me your wit is honed
to killing sharpness.
But I never catch
you simply smiling, anymore.

BORN THAT WAY

As far as possible, she strove
for them all. Arching her small
frame and grunting
prettily, her
fingers counting the roses
in the wallpaper.

Childhood whoring fitted her
for deceit. Daddy had been a
fondler. Soft lipped mouthings,
soft lapped rubbings.
A smile for pretty shoes,
a kiss could earn a dress.
And a private telephone
was worth the biggest old caress.

The neighbors and family friends
whispered she was seen
walking up and down the streets
when she was seventeen.
No one asked her reasons.
She couldn't even say.
She just took for granted
she was born that way.

As far as possible, she strove
for them all. Arching her small

frame and grunting
prettily, her
fingers counting the roses
in the wallpaper.

TELEVISED

Televised news turns
a half-used day into
a waste of desolation.
If nothing wondrous preceded
the catastrophic announcements,
certainly nothing will follow, save
the sad-eyed faces of
bony children,
distended bellies making
mock at their starvation.
Why are they always
Black?
Whom do they await?
The lamb-chop flesh
reeks and cannot be
eaten. Even the
green peas roll on my plate
unmolested. Their innocence
matched by the helpless
hope in the children's faces.
Why do Black children
hope? Who will bring
them peas and lamb chops
and one more morning?

NOTHING MUCH

But of course you were
always nothing. No thing.
A red-hot rocket, patriotically
bursting in my
veins. Showers of stars—cascading stars
behind closed eyelids. A
searing brand across my
forehead. Nothing of importance.
A four-letter word stenciled
on the flesh of my inner
thigh.
Stomping through my brain's
mush valleys. Strewing a
halt of new loyalties.

My life, so I say
        nothing much.

GLORY FALLS

Glory falls around us
as we sob
a dirge of
desolation on the Cross
and hatred is the ballast of
the rock
    which lies upon our necks
    and underfoot.
We have woven
    robes of silk
    and clothed our nakedness
    with tapestry.
From crawling on this
    murky planet's floor
    we soar beyond the
    birds and
    through the clouds
    and edge our way from hate
    and blind despair and
    bring honor
    to our brothers, and to our sisters cheer.
We grow despite the
    horror that we feed
    upon our own
    tomorrow.
We grow.

LONDON

If I remember correctly,
London is a very queer place.
Mighty queer.
A million miles from
jungle, and the British
lion roars in the stone of
Trafalgar Square.
Mighty queer.
At least a condition
removed from Calcutta,
but old men in Islington and in
too-large sweaters dream
of the sunrise days
of the British Raj.
Awfully queer.
Centuries of hate divide St. George's
channel and the Gaels,
but plum-cheeked English boys drink
sweet tea and grow to fight
for their Queen.
Mighty queer.

SAVIOR

Petulant priests, greedy
centurions, and one million
incensed gestures stand
between your love and me.

Your *agape* sacrifice
is reduced to colored glass,
vapid penance, and the
tedium of ritual.

Your footprints yet
mark the crest of
billowing seas but
your joy
fades upon the tablets
of ordained prophets.

Visit us again, Savior.

Your children, burdened with
disbelief, blinded by a patina
of wisdom,
carom down this vale of
fear. We cry for you
although we have lost
your name.

MANY AND MORE

There are many and more
who would kiss my hand,
taste my lips,
to my loneliness lend
their bodies' warmth.

I have want of a friend.

There are few, some few,
who would give their names
and fortunes rich
or send first sons
to my ailing bed.

I have need of a friend.

There is one and only one
who will give the air
from his failing lungs
for my body's mend.

And that one is my love.

THE NEW HOUSE

What words
have smashed against
these walls,
crashed up and down these
halls,
lain mute and then drained
their meanings out and into
these floors?

What feelings, long since
dead,
streamed vague yearnings
below this ceiling
light?
In some dimension,
which I cannot know,
the shadows of
another still exist. I bring my
memories, held too long in check,
to let them here shoulder
space and place to be.

And when I leave to
find another house,
I wonder what among
these shades will be
left of me.

OUR GRANDMOTHERS

She lay, skin down on the moist dirt,
the canebrake rustling
with the whispers of leaves, and
loud longing of hounds and
the ransack of hunters crackling the near branches.

She muttered, lifting her head a nod toward freedom,
I shall not, I shall not be moved.

She gathered her babies,
their tears slick as oil on black faces,
their young eyes canvassing mornings of madness.
Momma, is Master going to sell you
from us tomorrow?

Yes.
Unless you keep walking more
and talking less.
Yes.
Unless the keeper of our lives
releases me from all commandments.
Yes.
And your lives,
never mine to live,
will be executed upon the killing floor of innocents.

Unless you match my heart and words,
saying with me,

I shall not be moved.

In Virginia tobacco fields,
leaning into the curve
on Steinway
pianos, along Arkansas roads,
in the red hills of Georgia,
into the palms of her chained hands, she
cried against calamity,
You have tried to destroy me
and though I perish daily,

I shall not be moved.

Her universe, often
summarized into one black body
falling finally from the tree to her feet,
made her cry each time in a new voice.
All my past hastens to defeat,
and strangers claim the glory of my love,
Iniquity has bound me to his bed,

yet, I must not be moved.

She heard the names,
swirling ribbons in the wind of history:
nigger, nigger bitch, heifer,
mammy, property, creature, ape, baboon,
whore, hot tail, thing, it.
She said, But my description cannot
fit your tongue, for
I have a certain way of being in this world,

and I shall not, I shall not be moved.

No angel stretched protecting wings
above the heads of her children,
fluttering and urging the winds of reason
into the confusion of their lives.
They sprouted like young weeds,
but she could not shield their growth
from the grinding blades of ignorance, nor
shape them into symbolic topiaries.
She sent them away,
underground, overland, in coaches and
shoeless.
When you learn, teach.
When you get, give.
As for me,

I shall not be moved.

She stood in midocean, seeking dry land.
She searched God's face.
Assured,
she placed her fire of service
on the altar, and though
clothed in the finery of faith,
when she appeared at the temple door,
no sign welcomed
Black Grandmother. Enter here.

Into the crashing sound,
into wickedness, she cried,
No one, no, nor no one million
ones dare deny me God. I go forth
alone, and stand as ten thousand.

The Divine upon my right
impels me to pull forever
at the latch on Freedom's gate.

The Holy Spirit upon my left leads my
feet without ceasing into the camp of the
righteous and into the tents of the free.

These momma faces, lemon-yellow, plum-purple,
honey-brown, have grimaced and twisted
down a pyramid of years.
She is Sheba and Sojourner,
        Harriet and Zora,
        Mary Bethune and Angela,
        Annie to Zenobia.

She stands
before the abortion clinic,
confounded by the lack of choices.
In the Welfare line,
reduced to the pity of handouts.
Ordained in the pulpit, shielded
by the mysteries.
In the operating room,
husbanding life.
In the choir loft,
holding God in her throat.
On lonely street corners,
hawking her body.
In the classroom, loving the
children to understanding.

Centered on the world's stage,
she sings to her loves and beloveds,
to her foes and detractors:

However I am perceived and deceived,
however my ignorance and conceits,
lay aside your fears that I will be undone,

for I shall not be moved.

PREACHER, DON'T SEND ME

Preacher, don't send me
when I die
to some big ghetto
in the sky
where rats eat cats
of the leopard type
and Sunday brunch
is grits and tripe.

I've known those rats
I've seen them kill
and grits I've had
would make a hill,
or maybe a mountain,
so what I need
from you on Sunday
is a different creed.

Preacher, please don't
promise me
streets of gold
and milk for free.
I stopped all milk
at four years old
and once I'm dead
I won't need gold.

I'd call a place
pure paradise

where families are loyal
and strangers are nice,
where the music is jazz
and the season is fall.
Promise me that
or nothing at all.

FIGHTIN' WAS NATURAL

Fightin' was natural,
hurtin' was real,
and the leather like lead
on the end of my arm
was a ticket to ride
to the top of the hill.
                    Fightin' was real.

The sting of the ointment
and scream of the crowd
for blood in the ring,
and the clangin' bell cuttin'
clean through the
cloud in my ears.
                    Boxin' was real.

The rope at my back
and the pad on the floor,
the smack of four hammers,
new bones in my jaw,
the guard in my mouth,
my tongue startin' to swell.
Fightin' was livin'.
Boxin' was real.
Fightin' was real.
                    Livin' was . . . hell.

LOSS OF LOVE

The loss of love and youth
and fire came raiding,
riding,
a horde of plunderers
on one caparisoned steed,
sucking up the sun drops,
trampling the green shoots
of my carefully planted years.

The evidence: thickened waist and
leathery thighs, which triumph
over my fallen insouciance.

After fifty-five
the arena has changed.
I must enlist new warriors.
My resistance,
once natural as raised voices,
importunes in the dark.
Is this battle worth the candle?
Is this war worth the wage?

May I not greet age
without a grouse, allowing
the truly young to own
the stage?

SEVEN WOMEN'S BLESSED ASSURANCE

1

One thing about me,
I'm little and low,
find me a man
wherever I go.

2

They call me string bean
'cause I'm so tall.
Men see me,
they ready to fall.

3

I'm young as morning
and fresh as dew.
Everybody loves me
and so do you.

4

I'm fat as butter
and sweet as cake.
Men start to tremble
each time I shake.

5

I'm little and lean,
sweet to the bone.
They like to pick me up
and carry me home.

6

When I passed forty
I dropped pretense,
'cause men like women
who got some sense.

7

Fifty-five is perfect,
so is fifty-nine,
'cause every man needs
to rest sometime.

IN MY MISSOURI

In my Missouri
I had known a mean man
A hard man
A cold man
Gutting me and killing me
Was an Ice man
A tough man
A man.

So I thought I'd never meet a sweet man
A kind man
A true man
One who in darkness you can feel secure man
A sure man.
A man.

But Jackson, Mississippi, has some fine men
Some strong men
Some black men
Walking like an Army were the sweet men
The brown men
The men.

In Oberlin, Ohio, there were nice men
Just men
And fair men
Reaching out and healing were the warm men
Were good men
The men.

Now I know that there are good and bad men
Some true men
Some rough men
Women, keep on searching for your own man
The best man
For you man
The man.

THEY ASK WHY

A certain person wondered why
a big strong girl like me
wouldn't keep a job
which paid a normal salary.
I took my time to lead her
and to read her every page.
Even minimal people
can't survive on minimal wage.

A certain person wondered why
I wait all week for you.
I didn't have the words
to describe just what you do.
I said you had the motion
of the ocean in your walk,
and when you solve my riddles
you don't even have to talk.

AILEY, BALDWIN, FLOYD, KILLENS, AND MAYFIELD

When great trees fall,
rocks on distant hills shudder,
lions hunker down
in tall grasses,
and even elephants
lumber after safety.

When great trees fall
in forests,
small things recoil into silence,
their senses
eroded beyond fear.

When great souls die,
the air around us becomes
light, rare, sterile.
We breathe, briefly.
Our eyes, briefly,
see with
a hurtful clarity.
Our memory, suddenly sharpened,
examines,
gnaws on kind words
unsaid,
promised walks
never taken.

Great souls die and
our reality, bound to

them, takes leave of us.
Our souls,
dependent upon their
nurture,
now shrink, wizened.
Our minds, formed
and informed by their
radiance,
fall away.
We are not so much maddened
as reduced to the unutterable ignorance
of dark, cold
caves.

And when great souls die,
after a period peace blooms,
slowly and always
irregularly. Spaces fill
with a kind of
soothing electric vibration.
Our senses, restored, never
to be the same, whisper to us.
They existed. They existed.
We can be. Be and be
better. For they existed.

Other works by Maya Angelou

And Still I Rise
Poems by Maya Angelou

'Maya Angelou writes from the heart and her language rings clear and true . . . Whether joyful, sad or playful, her poems speak with delicacy and depth of feeling' — *Publishers Weekly*

Maya Angelou's poetry — lyrical and dramatic, exuberant and playful — speaks of love, longing, partings; of Saturday night partying, and the smells and sounds of southern cities; of freedom and shattered dreams. 'The caged bird sings/ with a fearful trill/ of things unknown/ but longed for still / and his tune is heard/ on distant hill/ for the caged bird/ sings of freedom.' Of her poetry, *Kirkus Review* has written, 'It is just as much a part of her autobiography as *I Know Why the Caged Bird Sings, Gather Together in My Name, Singin' and Swingin' and Gettin' Merry Like Christmas*, and *Heart of a Woman*.'

Just Give Me a Cool Drink of Water 'Fore I Diiie
Poems by Maya Angelou

'Maya Angelou liberates and exhilarates through her magical, lyrical, mystical medium — poetry' — *Mary Bryce, Tribune*

From the best-selling author of *And Still I Rise* comes a marvellous new collection of poetry, published on her sixtieth birthday. Poems of love and regret, of racial strife and confrontation, songs of the people and songs of the heart — all are charged with Maya Angelou's zest for life and her rage at injustice. Lyrical, tender poems of longing, wry glances at betrayal and isolation combine with a fierce insight into 'hate and hateful wrath' in an unforgettable picture of the hope and concerns of one of America's finest contemporary writers.

Maya Angelou's Five Volumes of Autobiography

I Know Why the Caged Bird Sings

'Verve, nerve and joy in her own talents effervesce throughout this book' — *Julia O'Faolain*

'It's humour, even in the face of appalling discrimination, is robust. Autobiographical writing at its very best' — *Philip Oakes*

In this first volume of her extraordinary autobiography, Maya Angelou beautifully evokes her childhood in the American South of the 1930s. She and her brother live with their grandmother, in Stamps, Arkansas, where Maya learns the power of the 'whitefolks' at the other end of town. A visit to her adored mother ends in tragedy when Maya is raped by her mother's lover. But her extraordinary sense of wholeness emerges; she discovers the pleasures of dance and drama and gives birth to a treasured son.

Gather Together in My Name

'She has warmth and humour and a sense of wholeness and content that glows through — *Polly Toynbee*

'Exceptional . . . should have been published here long ago' — *Paul Bailey, Observer*

In this moving sequel to her bestselling *I Know Why the Caged Bird Sings*, the war is over and Maya has given birth to a son. Unemployed, isolated, she embarks on a series of brief lonely affairs and transient jobs — in shops, restaurants and nightclubs. Finally she turns to prostitution and the world of narcotics. But even in great adversity, Maya Angelou invests life with the remarkable sense of richness that has won her such an enormous following.

Singin' and Swingin' and Gettin' Merry Like Christmas

'She sees everything with an eye full of relish' — *Hilary Bailey, Guardian*

At twenty-one Maya Angelou's life has a double focus — music and her son. Working in a record store to support both, she is on the edge of new worlds: marriage: show business and, in 1954, a triumphant tour of Europe and North Africa as feature dancer with *Porgy and Bess*. There are setbacks and disappointments, but energy and a profound confidence in her ability to survive keep Maya buoyant. A joyful celebration of music and dance, travel and friendship, this is the third volume of Maya Angelou's marvellous autobiography.

The Heart of a Woman

'Loving the world, Maya Angelou also knows its cruelty and offers up her autobiography as an extraordinary mixture of innocence and depravity, of elegy and celebration' – *Nicci Gerrard, New Statesman*

Maya Angelou leaves California for a new life in New York, where she becomes immersed in the world of Black writers and artists in Harlem. Increasingly active in the Black rights movement, she is appointed Northern Coordinator to Martin Luther King. Her personal life is as tempestuous as ever: swept off her feet by Vusumze Make, South African freedom fighter, she marries him after a whirlwind courtship. They go to Egypt, where the marriage fails but her career blossoms. Holding the book together is Maya's absorbing account of her relationship with her son, as, with pain and joy, she watches him grow up to find his own identity.

All God's Children Need Travelling Shoes

'Maya Angelou has an amazing ability to take readers into her personal maze and lead them out again feeling refreshed and even jubilant' — *Clancy Sigal, Guardian*

Maya Angelou emigrates to Ghana, only to discover that 'you can't go home again'. Initially she experiences the joy of being Black in a Black country, certain that Africa must be her Promised Land. But Ghana leads its own paradoxical life: she finds official sexism but loving female friendship; Black solidarity but distrust of Black Americans. Through her circumstances of her new life — an affair with a seductive Malian, her son's near-tragic accident, politics, partying — her myth of 'Mother Africa' is dismantled. Encountering the country on its own terms, she comes to a new awareness of herself, of slavery and Black betrayal, of civil rights and mothering.

Virago publishes all five volumes of Maya Angelou's autobiography.